The Art and Science of Skateboarding

Monika Davies

✳ **Smithsonian**

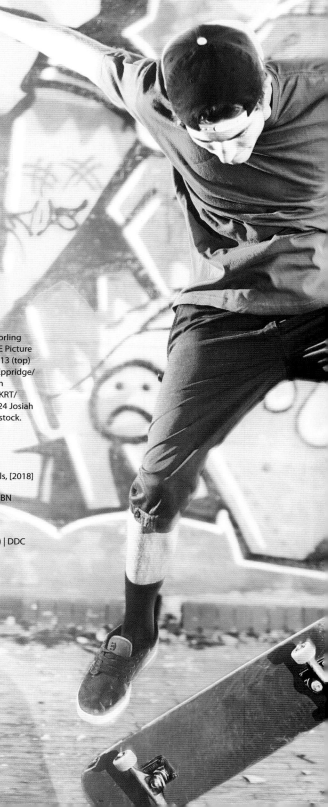

Contributing Author

Allison Duarte

Consultants

Jeffrey Brodie
Supervisory Museum Program Specialist
Lemelson Center for the Study of Invention & Innovation
National Museum of American History

Stephanie Anastasopoulos, M.Ed.
TOSA, STREAM Integration
Solana Beach School District

Publishing Credits

Rachelle Cracchiolo, M.S.Ed., *Publisher*
Conni Medina, M.A.Ed., *Managing Editor*
Diana Kenney, M.A.Ed., NBCT, *Content Director*
Véronique Bos, *Creative Director*
Robin Erickson, *Art Director*
Michelle Jovin, M.A., *Associate Editor*
Mindy Duits, *Senior Graphic Designer*
Smithsonian Science Education Center

Image Credits: p.4 Anatoliy Karlyuk/Shutterstock; p.7 (top, both) Dorling Kindersley/UIG/Bridgeman Images; p.12 (top) Ralph Morse/ The LIFE Picture Collection/Getty Images; p.12 (bottom) Pictorial Press Ltd/Alamy; p.13 (top) SZ Photo/Kurt Schraudenbach/Bridgeman Images; p.14 (right) Bill Eppridge/ The LIFE Picture Collection/Getty Images; p.15 Moviestore collection Ltd/Alamy; pp.16–17 Aurora Photos/Alamy; p.17 Charles Trainor Jr./KRT/ Newscom; p.18 Evan Hurd/Alamy; pp.20–21 (top, all) Lee Aucoin; p.24 Josiah True/ WENN/Newscom; all other images from iStock and/or Shutterstock.

Library of Congress Cataloging-in-Publication Data

Names: Davies, Monika, author.
Title: The art and science of skateboarding / Monika Davies.
Description: Huntington Beach, California : Teacher Created Materials, [2018]
 | Audience: Grades: 4 to 6. | Includes index. |
Identifiers: LCCN 2018018118 (print) | LCCN 2018024503 (ebook) | ISBN
 9781493869572 (E-book) | ISBN 9781493867172 (Paperback)
Subjects: LCSH: Skateboarding--Juvenile literature. | Sports
 sciences--Juvenile literature.
Classification: LCC GV859.8 (ebook) | LCC GV859.8 .D384 2018 (print) | DDC
 796.22--dc23
LC record available at https://lccn.loc.gov/2018018118

Smithsonian

Teacher Created Materials

5301 Oceanus Drive
Huntington Beach, CA 92649-1030
www.tcmpub.com
ISBN 978-1-4938-6717-2

Table of Contents

Editor's Note: Readers should always wear protective gear when skateboarding, including helmets that fit correctly, wrist guards, kneepads, elbow pads, and practical shoes. Always use quality skateboards to prevent injuries.

The Skate Park

Welcome to a community skate park! This space has ramps, stairs, and rails, and it's packed full of skaters. Some skaters zip past, rolling down basins quickly. Others swing by, hopping onto ledges and skating along edges with focused balance. One skater rockets down the pavement in a straight line. She bends her knees and jumps—lifting toward the sky—while her skateboard stays "attached" to her feet!

Everyone here has different skill levels. Even so, there's a sense of community. Beginners learn from the more experienced skaters. Long-time skaters work together to practice new tricks. As long as you're willing to try—and fall a time or two—the world of skateboarding is open to you.

Skaters are a welcoming group. They also cheer for creativity. Throughout history, skateboarding has gone through ups and downs. But skateboarding has remained a form of self-expression. For skaters, tricks are an art form—one they will never tire of perfecting and reinventing.

There is a lot to explore in the skateboarding world! So, are you ready to drop in?

Tony Hawk was a champion skateboarder, whose most famous trick was the 900 (2½ turns). Hawk is widely believed to be the first skater to ever land that trick.

The Basics of the Board

At first glance, skateboards have a simple design. They're just wooden boards with wheels, right? Actually, skateboards are more than they first appear to be. Even simple boards have a lot of clever design elements. Each **aspect** has been finely tuned over the years through trial and error.

ARTS

The Art of Grip Tape

Grip tape has a grainy surface that feels like sandpaper. This tape does exactly as its name suggests: it helps skaters grip the board. Skaters use grip tape and paint to create their own unique designs. These designs range from simple to inventive and can help skaters express themselves artistically.

A builder glues together plies of wood.

A builder traces the shape of a board onto plies of wood.

The Deck

The **anatomy** of a skateboard breaks into three parts—the deck, the wheels, and the trucks. The wooden plank that skateboarders stand on is the deck.

Today, decks are made of sugar maple wood. For years, **engineers** experimented with different materials for a skateboard's base. In the past, decks were made of aluminum or plastic. But maple wood has become the first-choice material for decks. This is due to the wood's strength and **elasticity**. Maple wood bends easily. This lets skateboard builders mold the deck.

A deck is usually made of seven plies, or layers, of wood. The layers are pressed tightly together using glue. The glue then dries, and the deck is shaped into the curved form people are used to seeing.

Skateboard decks come in several styles. However, most styles fall into two categories. The first category is the shortboard. True to its name, this board is the shortest style on the market, and it is also the most popular, recognizable style. The shortboard is built for tricks and jumps since it is the lightest of all boards.

The deck of a shortboard has a unique, concave design, which tilts up at the edges of the deck, as well as at the nose and tail of the board. This shape serves two purposes. First, the shape makes the board stronger. Second, it makes the board easier to control. The shape is also crucial to completing many well-known skateboarding tricks.

In contrast, the longboard is designed for travel. The longboard is the second category. Nicknamed "cruisers," these boards can glide down roads smoothly. The boards also turn corners with less effort. Longboards have longer decks, which can accommodate larger wheels.

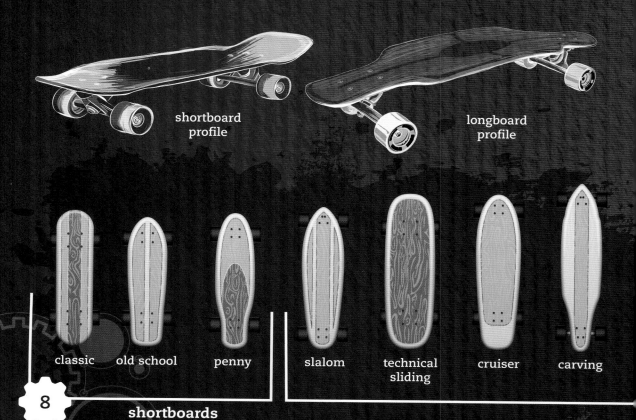

shortboard profile

longboard profile

classic   old school   penny   slalom   technical   cruiser   carving
                                                 sliding

These skaters ride shortboards at a park.

freeriding   cruising   long distance   speedboard   boardwalking   surf style

The Wheels

While decks are the support system of skateboards, wheels are what make them roll. Over the years, skateboard wheels have gone through many changes. Early on, people tried many different materials, all with little success.

Polyurethane (pah-lee-YOOR-uh-theyn) wheels smoothed out early problems—literally. Polyurethane is a type of plastic. Polyurethane wheels were introduced in the 1970s and led to a smoother (and slower) ride. The texture of the wheels provided more grip and made skating safer.

Today, polyurethane is still the top wheel choice. Skateboards come equipped with four of these tough, **durable** wheels. But skaters can choose the size, shape, and hardness they need for their specific skating styles.

The Trucks

The final piece of the skateboard puzzle is the trucks. Trucks are a board's steering system. They are frames made of aluminum or other metals. These frames direct a board's wheels in swinging curves, which help a skater control their route while riding.

While hidden from view, trucks are an **essential** part of a skateboard. This system allows skaters to control their direction by leaning. Leaning to the right means a skateboard will also go to the right. Leaning to the left means a skateboard will also go to the left.

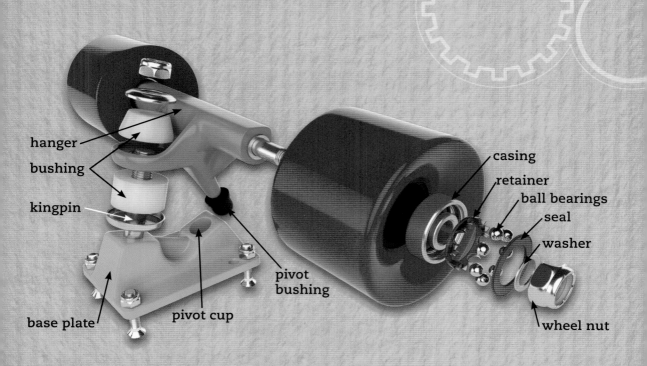

hanger

bushing

kingpin

base plate

pivot cup

pivot bushing

casing

retainer

ball bearings

seal

washer

wheel nut

Highs and Lows

Trucks come in different heights. The height difference between the two is just a couple of millimeters, but these tiny changes make a big difference. A low truck means a skateboard is lower to the ground, which makes it more stable. A high truck is heavier, but it lifts the skateboard higher above the ground. Some people believe this helps skaters jump higher. Each height has been engineered for a specific riding style.

A Broad Board History

Over the decades, skateboards have changed their shape, build, wheels—and even purpose! Roll back, and take a look at the board's history.

1950s: The Modern Board Hits the Scene

Skateboards were first made in the 1940s from wooden boxes. But it wasn't until the '50s that California surfers created modern skateboards. Ocean tides are not always surf-ready, so on bad surf days, surfers looked for other ways to ride. This jumpstarted the idea of "sidewalk surfing."

The first skateboards had a basic set-up. They were wooden planks with roller skate wheels attached. People rode down boardwalks on this new invention. Riding boards with wheels mimicked the motion of riding waves.

A child makes a skateboard from an orange crate in 1947.

1960s: Room for Improvement

A group of boys competes in a skateboarding contest in 1962.

Larry Stevenson was a California lifeguard. From his lifeguard tower, Stevenson saw skaters riding on wobbly, homemade boards. He knew they could be improved.

Two key designs were thanks to him. First, he made boards that rolled on clay wheels. These wheels had a bit more traction, which made it easier for skaters to stop and turn. Second, he won a patent for his new design—the kicktail. This design revolutionized skateboarding and paved the way for new tricks.

Two friends ride a skateboard in the 1950s.

Sidewalk
Surfing

Clay
Wheels

1950s

1960s

Before clay wheels, the first skateboards had steel wheels! These wheels made for a dangerous ride as they spun down roads with little to no traction.

1965: Board Sales Crash

Skateboarding was a rising sport. But, in 1965, its rise skidded to a halt. Safety was an ongoing issue for the sport. Medical experts branded the sport as a "menace." Many stores stopped selling skateboards. Parents cancelled skateboard orders for their kids, and sales plummeted.

1972: Playing with Poly

In 1972, a man named Frank Nasworthy changed the future of skateboarding. He did it with one simple idea—polyurethane wheels.

Roller skate wheels were already made of polyurethane. Nasworthy used the plastic to make skateboard wheels. It was a success! These new wheels made skateboarding smoother and safer. Polyurethane wheels are still used.

A group of skaters crash in 1965.

14

1975: The "Z-Boys" Zip In

In 1975, a group of 11 boys and 1 girl, called the Z-boys, performed at a contest. They thrilled the crowd with their edgy, fearless tricks. Before, people thought of skateboarding as a tame sport. But, the Z-boys' tricks showed the world a new side. Their style would end up defining the sport for years to come. Today, the Z-boys are seen as legends in the skateboarding world.

In the early 1960s, most skaters either raced downhill or performed freestyle. *Freestyle* refers to tricks done on flat land.

Z-boys member Peggy Oki skates downhill.

"Menace" Sport

Poly Wheels

"Z-boys" Legends

1965

1972

1975

1976-78: New Terrains

California suffered a **drought** in the late 1970s. To save water, many swimming pools were drained. These empty concrete basins became new grounds to be explored. Skaters began skating up the sides of empty pools. For years, skaters had only ridden on horizontal ground. With these pools, they had vertical options too!

In the 1970s, skaters also rode at construction sites. Giant sewer pipes let them try out new vertical tricks. This unsafe (and illegal) practice had mainly died out by the 1980s.

Getting Vertical

Ollie Invented

Urban Boarding

1976

1978

1980s

1978: Ollie Origins

In 1978, Alan "Ollie" Gelfand came up with a way to make his board fly. By skating down ramps and pools, he could jump in the air and take his board with him! This trick became known as an ollie. Three years later, Rodney Mullen created a way to do an ollie without needing a ramp. With this, the flat-ground ollie—and street tricks—were born.

1980s: An Underground Movement

Skateboarding kept growing as new concrete skate parks opened. But by the 1980s, insurance rates for the parks were getting too high. Parks were designed poorly and too many people were getting injured.

Still, dedicated skaters kept riding. Smaller skateboarding companies opened. They made and tested new styles of boards. Unsafe skate parks pushed skaters out of parks and into streets, as skateboarding became more **urban**.

Gelfand skates in a bowl in 2004.

1995: The First X Games

In 1995, skateboarding finally got picked up by the **mainstream media**. ESPN hosted the first X Games. The X Games are a sports festival which highlights **alternative** sports.

The televised games were a huge event. The games led to a huge increase in skateboarding's audience. This was key to changing public opinion of the sport. Viewers watched skaters complete difficult tricks. For many, it was the first time they'd seen the sport in action.

Before the X Games, skateboarding had an outsider profile. Not many people knew about it. After the X Games, it gained fame as a professional sport.

Shown on TV — 1995

Common Sport — 2000s

Lyn-Z Adams Hawkins skates in the X Games.

2000s: A Common Sight

Today, it's easy to catch a glimpse of a skater on a board. Skate parks are a common sight. Skaters can find a wide selection of boards at any sporting goods store. It's easier than ever to start skateboarding.

Once, skateboarding was an unconventional hobby. Now, the sport is widely accepted. And skateboarding is still driven by the creativity of skaters!

An architect designs a skate park on her computer.

TECHNOLOGY

Designing the Perfect Skate Park

Over time, empty swimming pools gave way to concrete skate parks. These parks are products of technology. Engineers use software to design skate parks. They can create 3-D models of a park, design areas for tricks, and can even inspect soil under a park. Park builders can build a virtual skate park before ever breaking ground.

Tricks: A How-To Guide

Tricks are part of the skateboarding craft, and they are all made possible by forces and motion. Examine how to complete three essential tricks: the kick turn, the ollie, and the grind.

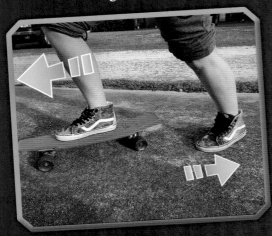 

How to Kick Turn

The ollie has defined skateboarding, but most beginner skaters should first learn the kick turn. The kick turn is the most basic trick. It is when a skater pushes down on the tail of their board, placing pressure on the back wheels. The force lifts the nose of the board, and the skater then uses the motion of their body to spin the board. Basically, a kick turn helps a skater change direction! Kick turns can be completed at any angle.

Kick turns are an essential trick in skateboarding. Kick turns require skaters to have a solid sense of balance. Practicing kick turns will help skaters stay steady on their boards. This trick also helps beginners learn how to move *with* the motion of their boards, not *against* it.

MATHEMATICS

Kick Turn Angles

When beginners try kick turns, they may only be able to swing their boards in small angles. But over time, they may learn to make 180-degree turns—or even 360-degree turns! What does that mean? A quarter turn equals a 90-degree angle, while a half turn is 180 degrees. And a full turn is 360 degrees.

360°

90°

180°

How to Ollie

Mastering the ollie is high on most beginning skaters' to-do lists. The ollie is a trick in which a skater jumps high and their board jumps with them! At first look, this trick seems impossible, but practice makes it achievable.

To ollie, a skater must stand the right way on their board. Their back foot should rest on the tail of the board, while their front foot is in the middle.

Next, the skater bends their knees, slamming their back foot onto the tails—with as much force as possible—while jumping into the air. This one fluid motion takes a lot of practice to get right.

steps for an ollie

step 1

step 2

step 3

As the jump begins, the skater slides their front foot up their board, which pulls them up higher. Then, the skater pulls their knees to their chest as they level out.

Finally, gravity pulls the skater (and the board) back to the ground. As they land on the ground, the skater's knees bend again, absorbing the impact of the landing.

It takes time and effort to conquer this trick! But once mastered, the ollie lets a skater leapfrog into trickier jumps.

step 4

step 5

SCIENCE

The Science Behind an Ollie

While the ollie may seem to defy gravity, this trick happens because of science. When skaters bend their knees, they **exert** a force on the tails of their boards. The more skaters bend, the greater the force and the higher the jumps. The force on the tails causes the noses to pop up. These forces work together to push against gravity and lift skaters up into the air.

How to Grind

Once a skater can kick turn and ollie effortlessly, they can tackle the grind. The grind is a trick that makes use of a skater's environment.

Grinding is when a skater slides along an edge, such as a curb or rail, using a board's trucks. The most basic grind is known as a 50-50, which is when a skater grinds along the middle of a board's trucks.

The first step to completing a grind is to pick an edge. Most skaters begin with ledges. Ledges are easily found in skate parks, where edges are often straight and lined with metal.

Next, skaters back up from a ledge, giving themselves a fair amount of distance. Then, they ride up to the ledge, building speed, and ollie up onto it. Once they land on the ledge, the skaters grind, or slide, along it while keeping their weight balanced. At the tail end of a ledge, skaters pop off, landing level on the ground in one motion.

In the skateboarding world, each trick builds skills needed for the next. Once skaters know how to kick turn, ollie, and grind, they have built a foundation to learn tougher tricks.

The world record for the highest ollie is 114 centimeters (45 inches). The world record for the longest 50-50 grind is 62 meters (204 feet).

Jagger Eaton set the world record for the longest 50-50 grind in 2016.

A skateboarder performs a 50-50 grind.

25

Art in Motion

The world of skateboarding has changed a lot over the years. It is a sport that has struggled in the past. Today, the skateboarding world continues to grow. Unique skate parks interest new riders. These parks are great places for young skaters to learn and grow.

In skateboarding, creativity is encouraged. New tricks are regularly invented. Engineers look for interesting ways to shape skate parks. And designers look for ways to help skaters do more on their boards.

While skateboarding is not a team activity, skaters often have a support system in the community. Skaters are a tightly knit group who try to help one another. However, at the end of the day, skaters are their own decision makers. They decide which tricks they should try. And they alone decide how to push themselves to become better skaters.

Every day, skaters get new ideas. They express themselves through their tricks. This kind of creativity is what makes skateboarding more than a sport. It's what makes skateboarding art in motion!

A skater performs a boardslide grind on a pipe.

Skateboarding is now an Olympic® sport! The 2020 Summer Games in Tokyo mark the first time skaters can take home the gold for their tricks.

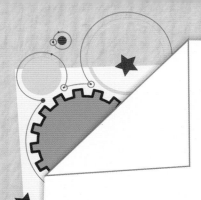

STEAM CHALLENGE

Define the Problem

Engineers consider many things when designing safe and unique skate parks. They test the size, angle, surface material, and shape of ramps so that skaters can use them to practice and invent tricks. Your task is to design and build a model of a new skate park for your community.

 Constraints: The design must be safe and useful for skaters. It must include at least three attractions where skaters can kick turn, ollie, and grind. There must be a safe area for both beginners and experts.

 Criteria: Your model must clearly show different areas of the park where tricks can be practiced safely.

Research and Brainstorm

What types of tools do engineers use to design skate parks? What attractions are popular for beginners? What attractions are popular for experts?

Design and Build

Sketch your park design. What purpose will each part serve? What materials will work best? Build the model.

Test and Improve

Test your model. Use a piece of a craft stick and your fingers to show how tricks should be performed. Did they work? How can you improve the park? Modify your design and try again.

Reflect and Share

How would you modify your attractions if almost all the people who visit your park are beginners? What were the biggest challenges you faced when designing your skate park?

Glossary

accommodate—have or provide room for something

alternative—existing outside of established society

anatomy—the parts that form or create something

aspect—feature of something

concave—having a shape similar to the inside of a bowl

drought—a long period of time in which there is little to no rain

durable—remaining in good condition over a period of time

elasticity—ability to be molded or changed

engineers—people who have scientific training and who design and build products, machines, systems, or structures

essential—necessary and extremely important

exert—use strength or ability to do something

mainstream media—radio stations, TV stations, and newspapers that deliver the thoughts and beliefs of the majority of people

menace—a danger or threat

mimicked—created the effect of something

patent—an official guarantee for an inventor to be the only one to make, use, and sell their invention

tame—dull; not exciting or interesting

tides—the regular upward and downward movements of the level of water

traction—the force that causes a moving thing to stick to the surface of what it is moving along

urban—relating to cities

Skateboard Time Line

Sidewalk Surfing — 1950s

Clay Wheels — 1960s

"Menace" Sport — 1965

Poly Wheels — 1972

"Z-boys" Legends — 1975

Index

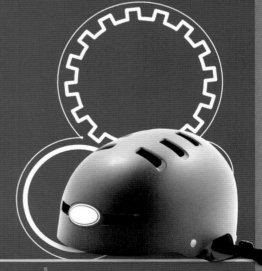

Getting Vertical	Ollie Invented	Urban Boarding	Shown on TV	Common Sport
1976	1978	1980s	1995	2000s

Do you want to work in skateboarding?
Here are some tips to get you started.

"To understand skateboarding, you just have to try it. In addition, sports, history, physics, mathematics, technology, and design all play a role in skateboarding. Study those subjects, and you can be part of skateboarding history." —*Jeffrey Brodie, Program Specialist*

"Skateboarding is not just about doing tricks. Native artists and filmmakers credit the sport with teaching them a successful work ethic. In addition, athleticism, fearlessness, and creativity are all traits that encompass skateboarding. If you have those traits, you can work in skateboarding—even if you never get on a board!" —*Betsy Gordon, Curator*